STRIPPED away

STRIPPED away

A WORKBOOK OF RESTORATION FOR MEN

Tammy R. Dickenson, L.P.C.

XULON PRESS

Xulon Press
2301 Lucien Way #415
Maitland, FL 32751
407.339.4217
www.xulonpress.com

ISBN-13: 978-1-6312-9454-9

This book is specifically designed to be used as a ten-week small group study, a therapeutic curriculum, or it can be presented in a retreat/intensive setting. This study can also be done individually if the opportunity for a group is unavailable.

DEDICATION

T o my boys, Ethan, Jake and Maxx, who have been my greatest gifts. I stand in agreement with every promise that God has spoken over your lives.

TABLE OF CONTENTS

INTRODUCTION TO STRIPPED away: a WORKBOOK OF RESTORATION FOR men

Restoration: bringing back to a redeemed or improved condition

This study is a God-initiative based on my own story of survival and, ultimately, victory. It is a leap of faith after God led me to create a study for men from the perspective of a helpmate. Specifically, this study is designed for men who work hard and have a heart for Jesus, men who have dreams and a calling but who have fallen into a trap of trying to balance their faith, family, and work. These same men are surviving but broken in their personal relationships and in their ability to be fully present with God. They are living in a pressure cooker and feel like they are being constantly measured and judged by those around them. They show up every day but are desperately missing the peace, joy, and contentment they have longed for their entire lives. These are men who want to stand for God but have gotten weary and overcome by the weight of this world. They are walking in the roles they have seen for generations with their own fathers, trying to overcome fear, insecurity, and inadequacy.

These men, like David, were once just broken little boys. This is not a sign of weakness as our world would say but a beginning point for becoming what God has called them to be. You see, God always uses broken people to do His most significant work. The ones who run out of strength and can no longer stand on their own two feet make great kingdom-changers. Remember when the Lord was ready to appoint a new king for Israel, He sent Samuel to Jesse's house because one of his sons was to be the chosen king. When Samuel arrived at the house, David's father Jesse did not even acknowledge David as he presented the rest of his sons as possible candidates. He believed the other sons were the only real choices for this position. It was only when God led Samuel to ask if there was another boy that Jesse even mentioned David (1 Sam. 16:12).

You see, even David's own earthly father was basing the selection of the king on outward appearances and strengths, while God was looking at David's heart. He saw what others did not; He saw the heart of a warrior. While David was in the field, he was talking with God; he was growing and getting stronger in his faith while protecting the sheep from fierce predators. His heart was being prepared to carry the mantle and responsibilities of a great king, being prepared to be the one brave enough to fight his giant Goliath. I believe today you are in a battle as well, facing your own giants and pressures of your daily responsibilities, still carrying the wounds of a young man but being prepared for significance in every area of your life.

This study is designed and created from years of experience as a counselor walking with men toward healthiness and godliness. It is designed to help men individually and in a group setting to be fully surrendered and ready to serve God in every area. It is also designed to give you permission to share your hurts and allow you to be more vulnerable. It is my hope that this process will encourage you to be more open and transparent with your wounds, have a willingness to share your testimony, and make an impact in the world around you.

This is not just a book or an idea; it is a God assignment given to me through the lens of my profession and my own brokenness. I have walked in hard and painful places in my life with deep wounds, longing to know that I am loved and valued. Every woman needs a man who knows his authority in the kingdom and who is able to demonstrate Christ-like love, placing her well-being above his very life. This same man as he walks in the power and authority of the cross provides a covering, protection, and a place of spiritual security for his family.

God gave me a vision and a workbook but most importantly a heart for men. I have found myself over the last twenty years being a sounding board and an advocate for men of all ages and walks of life. I have come to understand that it is the power of our testimonies and the broken parts of our lives that God can work most profoundly through. I believe that out of our deepest wounds will come our greatest calling and that the way we will defeat darkness in this world is, as Scripture states, with the blood of Jesus the Lamb and the word of our testimony. It is a privilege to share with you what God has shown me, and it is my sincere desire to walk in obedience as the helpmate He has called me to be. Thank you for trusting this process and taking this journey alongside of me.

Tammy

Assessment:

What is your most difficult struggle as a man?

_____

_____

_____

What is your greatest strength?

_____

_____

_____

What is your greatest weakness?

_____

_____

_____

How do you measure success?

_____

_____

_____

Is friendship important to you? How would you describe these relationships?

_____

_____

_____

What do you dream about?

_____

_____

_____

If I interviewed your family, what would they say about you?

_____

_____

_____

Have you thought about your funeral?

_____

_____

_____

Your obituary? What would you want it to say?

_____

_____

_____

How is your relationship with Jesus?

_____

_____

_____

Who holds you accountable?

_____

_____

_____

What is your greatest fear?

_____

_____

_____

Do you relax, rest, or be still? How? When?

_____

_____

_____

Where is the most beautiful, peaceful place you have ever been?

_____

_____

_____

What do you wish people knew about you but you could never tell them?

_____

_____

_____

PRINCIPLE 1: THE TRUTH ABOUT FEELINGS

ave you ever thought about how being emotionally healthy was related to your relationship with God? As a counselor, I have spent years being an advocate for emotional healthiness. I believe that just like having a relationship with God requires intentionality, so does managing one's emotional health. The way we naturally respond to our emotions many times is very unhealthy. Most of us were raised in families that were not very skilled in processing or validating the emotions that we all felt. I remember very early on being taught to put away my feelings and to just be nice. Can any of you relate? I think this tendency toward stuffing and repressing of emotion is especially taught and modeled for men in our culture. You see, the truth is that feelings are really just a natural part of who we are. They are not facts and should not be treated as such; they are also not to be dismissed and given no credibility. Feelings are natural and God-given; they literally flow through us all day long. That's their design to just be a part, along with our minds and wills, to create our souls.

Now ultimately as we are transformed by the Holy Spirit, the Spirit desires to take authority over our souls. This does not mean that we should repress or ignore our emotions. Feelings are not right or wrong or good or bad—they simply are. So many times we believe that it is alright to feel happiness or joy but not okay to feel anger or sadness. This is simply not true! A feeling is just a feeling. I encourage my clients to practice giving themselves permission to pay attention to and recognize what they feel about a given situation. I teach people to acknowledge what they feel without any judgment or condemnation. You see, if you begin to judge a feeling, trying not to feel something, it really has the reverse effect. The more you try not to feel it, the more it lingers and even can begin to take a deeper root in the heart. A feeling just needs to be felt, and many times, that is all that is required for it to pass through and for a person to move on from it. If I am angry with someone, it is always best to acknowledge this in my heart and let it flow through me. If it gets stuck or seems to linger, I can take it to God in prayer, and He can specifically help me work through any feeling, especially ones that are tied to an offense or a deep wound. I may even need to share my feelings with those with whom I am in relationship. This allows others to truly see my heart, and in this place of vulnerability, true intimacy and closeness can be found. So let's get this straight:

1) Feelings are not right or wrong.
2) Feelings are not a sign of weakness.
3) They are not facts, and we should not base our decisions strictly on them. We are designed to have our logic and emotions work together, overlapping in a healthy way to create a wise mind.
4) We can only change deeply-rooted, painful feelings by changing our thinking—by lining up our thinking to God's Word and identifying any lies that we believe.
5) Feelings are meaningful and bring color into our world. These feelings are the essence of the life experiences we have while on this earth. They may be beautiful, wonderful, or deeply painful. The idea that we can just decide which ones we will experience sounds good, right? We would just let all the happy feelings come and the painful ones just fall away. I wish it worked that way, but it just does not. The truth about life is that it is so beautiful and also brutal at the same time; this is a complete picture of what it means to be alive and human. Feelings allow us to experience life in a full and complete way. Think about a sunrise, seeing your child for the

first time, or falling in love. Or maybe think about getting angry when someone you love is mistreated, grieving the loss of a loved one, or a going through a divorce. All these feelings give a realistic account of the life that we walk through under the sun. The Bible says there is a place where every tear is wiped away and no pain is present. (Rev. 21:4). This beautiful place is heaven, and, yes, I definitely want to go there. Until then, we are called to experience each facet of life and have the faith to believe that God is in each beautiful sunset and in each devastating moment.

6) Sharing feelings in a safe and healthy way shows a willingness to be vulnerable, creating closeness and intimacy in relationship. It can also set up a bridge for healing as each person chooses to share his or her deepest feelings, both hurts and joys.

7) Avoidance of painful feelings actually puts Miracle-Gro on them and causes them to get more deeply-rooted and difficult. For instance, refusing to deal with the feeling of anger can lead to resentment, which can ultimately lead to bitterness. This avoidance also sets us up to engage in medicating or numbing-out behaviors in an attempt to not to feel something painful. Ultimately, if we will give ourselves permission to acknowledge a feeling, we can be set

free from the pain. If we refuse to empty out our hearts of deeply-rooted pain and the lies that may accompany them, we make no room for the Holy Spirit to fill us with His love, grace, and power.

8) Let's name some feelings—sadness, rejection, fear, anger, hurt, lust, love, joy, insecurity, guilt, shame, and excitement, just to name a few.

In summary, feelings are not our enemy as we have heard many times in our culture and even in our churches. They are designed to be experienced and then to flow through us. If we find ourselves stuck with a particular feeling, we can learn to respond to it in a healthy way. We can also take our feelings to God in prayer; sharing them with Him in a very vulnerable way allows Him to bring healing to our deepest and most painful wounds.

*Feelings List (see Appendix)

Principle 1: Homework

1) What were you taught growing up about feelings?

_____

_____

_____

2) Do you have certain feelings that you are currently struggling with? Would you mind sharing?

_____

_____

_____

3) Have you believed that feelings are a sign of weakness? How has this affected you in your current life?

_____

_____

_____

Prayer:

Lord Jesus, I thank you for creating me in Your image. God, I ask that You would forgive me for elevating logic over my emotions. Give me the ability to use my emotions and resonable thinking together as You designed. I choose to yield each of these parts of myself to Your Holy Spirit. I pray You will undo and redeem any faulty thinking I have about acknowledging and expressing my feelings. In Jesus's name, Amen.

Declaration:

Lord, I will stand as an aligned man. I will boldly surrender my heart and mind in a way that is pleasing to You. I will risk being seen and be willing to share my feelings with others as You prompt me. I will learn to walk with You as a loving servant, tender and strong, leading the ones I love according to Your truth.

2 Kings 20:5, Psalm 34:17-18, 2 Corinthians 1:3-4

PRINCIPLE 2:
managing emotions/
coping with pain

So now that you have given yourself permission to actually acknowledge feelings, let's really unpack this. You see, the idea with painful feelings is to acknowledge and allow them to flow through us and be laid at the foot of the cross. First let me say that managing your emotions in a healthy way is a skill. The truth is that dysfunction comes naturally to all of us because of the earth suits we wear. The tendency to react in an unhealthy and destructive manner is inside all of us.

So I want to talk about how we cope with our feelings/ frustrations in the most helpful and healing way. There is a difference between healthy and unhealthy coping behaviors. Let me explain.

Unhealthy Coping: These are coping strategies that involve quick fixes. They never resolve the hurt or pain but serve to medicate and numb a person. They remind me of the way pain medication stops a headache by dulling the pain receptors. The headache will usually go away on its own, but in the meantime, the medication covers the pain receptors so you do not feel it. These types of behaviors say to you that if you feel pain, you need to do whatever you can to avoid that feeling. In other words, if you start to feel overwhelmed, you must shut it down immediately. As we talked about in Principle 1, feelings are just designed to be felt, and then they can be released. These behaviors serve to keep the pain and lies locked deep inside,- functioning like a tightly-secured lid, keeping us filled with deeply-rooted pain and unresolved issues. It is human nature when we experience pain and it hurts to look for the quickest way possible to make the pain stop. These coping behaviors include drugs, alcohol, sex, pornography, perfectionism, compulsive working, overthinking, food, people pleasing, and distractions (phone, TV, computer).

These coping behaviors, although quick and effective in neutralizing pain, are only good for a short period of time. They are short-acting and over time require more and more of the behavior to sustain the same effect. They also have unfortunate side effects. They serve to keep our pain out of reach, buried deep inside and away from our Father's healing touch. You see, you cannot change what you refuse to acknowledge. Unhealthy coping mechanisms create a truckload of secondary consequences and are always shame-based. These behaviors are pleasure-based and while engaging in them we feel relief, but we can develop a dependency on these behaviors to manage life. These types of coping strategies many times cause our brains to release dopamine (a feel-good chemical), ultimately creating a craving within our systems to continue to apply these behaviors. Therefore, a person who is struggling with a painful emotion medicates to stop the pain, becomes dependent on the shame-based coping behavior, and actually compounds the original painful emotion.

Spiritual Consequences: These coping behaviors are unhealthy and set us up to believe that something counterfeit and false can really be our source of relief. These unhealthy coping behaviors will never provide lasting peace or safety. It is the work of the enemy to create a disconnect between our heads and hearts, a heart guard that convinces us that the cross is not enough and that we cannot fully trust God to heal our broken emotions. In other words, these counterfeit walls or guards serve to diminish the complete work of the Holy Spirit in our lives. They keep our pain covered and in the dark, the exact place that the enemy does his best work.

Garbage and rats: Many years ago, I read a book by Charles Kraft that described our emotions and the way the enemy uses the pain in our lives to destroy us. The metaphor he used was profound. He described unresolved pain and deep-seated negative beliefs as the garbage of our life. In other words, the garbage are the beliefs that we still hold onto that are opposite from what God says is true about us, the deep-seated lies that we have believed for many years. This garbage, if left unattended, can become deep issues within our emotions, thinking, and relationships. He went on to describe the spiritual rats that feed on the garbage. These are the specific spirits that attach and feed on the open door of our unresolved pain. In my own life, as a young girl, I experienced a traumatic event that terrified me. Now I was able to survive this event without any physical harm, but the emotional scar lasted for years. You see, in that moment, the doorway of fear, specifically the lie that I was not safe, swung open. It opened my heart to believe I was unsafe, and this belief kept me tied up in bondage to fear for much of my lifetime. In other words, the enemy began to tell me a lie. It was so overwhelming, and I had no idea how to stop the feelings, so I learned to manage fear in very unproductive and destructive way. This tormenting fear kept me reminded of my pain and whispered to me that God was really not able to keep me safe in any situation. The enemy used the proof of a one-time event to torment me for so many years! Yes, it is true I had gotten through this situation and had moved on, but I had never processed or emptied the lie out at the cross, allowing Jesus to completely heal me. The pain and the lie that I was unsafe and unprotected stayed locked deep inside my heart. Eventually, my mentors led me back to the root of this open door. I processed the pain, identified the lie, and told the enemy to leave. I had no idea that this block or tormenting fear was really a lie from the enemy.

Healthy Coping Behaviors: These are resolution-based practices that actually allow us to work through a painful or overwhelming emotion. They function like a spout, allowing us to pour out the hurt and empty the pain. They are not as fast-acting as the above-described coping strategies—they require a little more time to take effect. I compare it to a microwave meal or a home-cooked dinner that your grandmother prepared. The first is quicker and easier, but the second one is much more satisfying! These coping skills are not shame-based and actually participate with healthiness and godly principles. They are not addictive in nature, and they do not create a dependency or tendency toward compulsive behavior. They will typically set us up for healthy habits that actually make us feel more whole and complete. They cooperate with our ability to feel the pain and then release it appropriately.

Let's name a few:

prayer, reading the Bible, therapy, exercise, talking with a friend, journaling, walking in nature, visualization, praise and worship, and being creative.

Spiritual Benefits: When we allow ourselves to acknowledge and express our pain, it is emptied out. Healthy coping serves to resolve and empty our cups of the lies and pain that keep us stuck in the past. Once we find the courage to empty out our cup, the enemy's ability to accuse us and deceive us is very limited. As we release the garbage, the rats now have nothing to feed on! Our vessels get opened up, and there is now room for the Holy Spirit and the truth of God's Word to take full residency in our hearts, minds, and will. We will talk in Principle #6 about how many of these healthy coping skills will not only allow us to empty out the pain but lead us toward abiding and remaining in God's presence.

So in summary, situations that evoke painful or difficult feelings may require a set of behaviors to effectively manage the emotional response. Choosing to understand and develop healthy coping is a skill that will allow you to manage and resolve deep wounds. By you keeping your heart open and available, God is able to fill you with His truth and love. The unhealthy coping mechanisms keep us holding onto false or counterfeit places of safety. These behaviors, although effective for a short period of time, set us up for dependency and keep the Holy Spirit diminished in our lives. Our souls become filled with the counterfeit guards, and we have little room for His truth. The cups of our lives stay filled with our past pain, complicated by behaviors that keep us in shame.

> Ultimately, the goal is to deal with our deep pain by confessing it first to ourselves, then to God, and then to others. We must remove the old habit of holding onto counterfeit coping and replace it with behaviors that empty out the pain and promote healthiness. This gives the rats nothing to feed on, allowing our hearts to be filled with God's love and the healing power of the blood of Jesus (1 Peter 2:24).

Principle 2: Homework

1) Can you identify the ways that you typically cope with difficult emotions in your life? Would you classify these as healthy or unhealthy?

_____

_____

_____

2) How do the unhealthy coping strategies affect your self-esteem?

_____

_____

_____

3) Would you be willing to trade in your unhealthy coping for new healthy behaviors? Which ones would you like to give to God today?

_____

_____

_____

Prayer:

Heavenly Father, I thank you that You have no problem healing my broken heart. You know all my hurts and the greatest struggles in my life. I ask that You would forgive me for leaning on counterfeit, unhealthy coping behaviors. I thank you that Your cross is enough and that the blood of Jesus covers all my pain and shame. Please show me how to manage my emotions in a way that resolves the pain and leads me into a deeper relationship with You.

In Jesus's name, Amen.

Declaration:

I will stand intentionally, identifying and trading in unhealthy coping behaviors that function like a LID, keeping pain deeply rooted inside my heart. Instead, I will adopt healthy coping behaviors that act as SPOUTS, resolving and pouring out my hurts and pain at the foot of the cross. I choose to empty myself out so the Lord can make me completely free.

John 8:36, Psalm 91:14-15, 2 Corinthians 3:16-17

PRINCIPLE 3: THE LITTLE BOY IS DRIVING THE BUS

I want to talk about the importance of recognizing childhood wounds. Years ago, I was trained and taught by some of the best people on the planet. These were clinicians and psychologists by profession but ministers at heart. I was taught early on in my career as a therapist that if I wanted to understand the hearts of people, I needed to be able to understand the little boy or girl living inside their hearts. The wounds in all of our hearts usually began at the hands of those we loved the most when we were children. These are the formative years that really shape our perception of God, self, and others. This pain can many times linger and be deeply rooted inside of us. We really don't realize the effect that these painful internalized emotion can have on us as adults. There seems to be a mentality that as we grow up, we grow past our pain and somehow just become well-adjusted adults. That is actually not the way it works at all!

The internalized pain sits and resides in the deepest part of our hearts and minds. We very quickly figure out ways to bury the suffering, in hopes of stopping the pain. We believe that if we don't focus on it and we ignore it, that it will somehow go away. As we repress these emotions, the pain becomes more deeplyrooted and begins to effect all areas of our life. The truth is that every place we ignore the pain, it can cripple our growth in significant ways. You may be a fully mature person, but when it comes to certain areas, especially when triggered, you may find yourself responding very much like you did as a little boy. As we talked about earlier, these hurts cause us to believe lies about ourselves. Because the wounds are experienced in childhood, they remain intact and experienced just as a child would process the pain. This is why we hear about people being stuck in a certain phase in their life. Although they are grown up, they respond to others and see themselves from the same wounded eyes of that broken child.

The enemy is very cunning and cruel, always coming in at a vulnerable and traumatic moment when our hearts feel shattered. The enemy literally has an assignment over our lives the moment we are birthed into this world. He begins very strategically to go after our purpose and calling in the kingdom. There are very few people who would invite the enemy over to dinner or willingly entertain him in their presence. The enemy always thrives on working covertly and under the radar. He always looks for an open doorway of pain, typically during childhood. He speak lies and convinces us to question our Father's love and our identity in Christ. One of the ways we combat the enemy and avoid a lifetime of lies and deception is to adequately deal with our childhood pain. I believe that dealing with childhood wounds should not just be reserved for those courageous enough to seek therapy but should be a skill that we all learn as Christ followers.

When we are born again, we become indwelled by the Holy Spirit, and this Spirit desires to have authority over our emotions, minds, and wills. Unfortunately, the doorways in childhood and the lies set us up to doubt the goodness and love of God, therefore diminishing the Spirit's impact on our lives. The wounds of childhood are literally stored up and compiled in layers in our hearts and minds. This pain and the lies we believe keep our cup filled with beliefs about ourselves and others that are opposite from what our Heavenly Father says.

As I talked about in the earlier section, as a child, I felt so much fear due to what had happened to me. This situation was terrifying to me as a young person, causing me a great deal of fear in the moment. Although I was able to move past the painful memory and get to a more stable place, the doorway to fear and insecurity had been opened in my emotions and in the spirit realm. This began to cause me to believe I was not safe at all. Now, it was subtle at first, but over the years, it developed into an anxiety disorder and such tremendous fear. This fear in my heart became an open door for the spirit of fear to begin to have authority over my life for almost thirty-five years.

Now let me say, years after this traumatic event, I became saved and gave my heart to Jesus. I knew He had given His life for mine and I was owned by the Holy Spirit. Although the enemy could not have his complete way with me through the lies, he saw an open door to torment me. This torment kept me from being set completely free by God. It is important to examine your heart and give yourself permission to look at the wounds and broken places in your childhood. By doing so, you can empty out any of the garbage and lies that you are still believing and learn to walk in truth about who God says you are.

Principle 3: Homework

1) What were the wounds that you suffered as a young person? Can you identify the feelings that you developed due to this wounding?

_____

_____

2) What lies have you believed about yourself because of the hurt you experienced growing up? For example, I am not good enough, I am worthless, I am rejected, I am unsafe.

_____

_____

_____

Take some extra time to identify the pain from your past, especially the deepest wounds and earliest childhood pain.

_____

_____

_____

Prayer

> Lord, I come before You now with an
> open and humble heart. I invite You to
> reveal to me all the broken places in
> my childhood. Please come in and heal
> every part of my heart. I give You per-
> mission to search me, God, and know
> my heart, to test me and know my
> anxious thoughts (Ps. 139:23). Please
> reveal to me any place in my mind or
> heart that I have believed a lie from
> the enemy. I choose to empty myself
> of my old wounds and lay them down
> at the foot of Your cross. In Jesus's
> name, Amen.

Declaration:

I will stand as a man who boldly embraces every aspect
of my life. I will willingly allow God full access to every
part of my heart and my thinking. I will be like David,
asking God to use my broken and painful emotions, my
victories and failures, as stepping stones to becoming
the man He have called me to be. I will not allow shame,
inadequacy, fear, or the lies of the enemy to keep me
from walking in my true identity in Christ.

Jeremiah 29:11, Psalm 147:3, Revelation 21:4

Consider following the guide in the appendix for writing a letter from you to yourself as a little boy.

PRINCIPLE 4: FORGIVENESS, REPENTANCE, AND SOUL TIES

~

n ow that you have given yourself permission to look at your heart and really go deeply into the pain, let's allow the King of the world to do what He is only able to do. You see, it is so important to choose to invite Him into every area of your life. Empty out the pain and place the cross of Jesus at the scene of every place that your heart was shattered. He just wants to heal you and mend your broken heart. God is so good, and His blood is sufficient to completely make you free. I want to unpack an important principle that allows Jesus's love and truth to permeate our being more than anything else. This is the understanding and concept of forgiveness. Let's start with the definition:

Forgiveness: It is a verb, implying that it requires action.

1 To cease to feel resentment against an offender: To pardon
2 To give up resentment or grant relief from an owed debt

Scripture references:

Matthew 6:14-15, Ephesians 4:31-32, 2 Corinthians 2:10-11

Forgiveness is a word that stirs up a lot of emotion in people. It is such a hard concept to understand and get our arms around. On one hand, it seems simple— God says forgive, so I need to forgive. He also goes on to say that if we do not forgive others, He will not forgive our sins (Matt. 6:14-15). That scripture always gets my attention! I know I spent years believing that I had forgiven certain people, only to realize that I had buried the pain deep inside and covered it with a statement of, "Yes, I have forgiven them!" I came to understand that true forgiveness involves giving oneself permission to actually validate the pain. We must acknowledge the depth of the pain we have experienced with the person. This part of the equation was really never made clear to me over the years. I always resisted forgiveness because it seemed as if it was giving the person a free pass for what he or she had done to me. It was only after really digging into this idea that I came to understand that there really was a process to forgiveness. I am thankful for Neils Anderson's work and his book *Steps to Freedom in Christ* that helped me truly understand the power of forgiveness. It involves full realization and disclosure of the pain that the person caused you. It really is never the act that the person did to us that needs forgiving; it is the way the person made us feel during this experience. The feelings can linger years and years in our hearts. This act of betrayal or hurt can set the stage for deep offense and avoidance of the pain for decades. We literally build a wall around the pain and just go on with life as usual. Unfortunately, this wall that we use as protection becomes, when used by the enemy, a stronghold in our life. A stronghold is a habitual pattern of thought that keeps a belief deeply rooted and stuck in our soul. This wall is fortified when we hold onto unforgiveness and blocks God from fully setting us free. We remain in bondage and chains from the harm we have experienced. I once heard a saying that forgiveness doesn't make you weak—it sets you free! Forgiveness is so powerful. It allows us to live in the present, it connects us to our Father, and it opens doors to fully trust God and others again.

Truths about Forgiveness:

1) Forgiveness is a choice, a decision, not based on a feeling.
2) You agree to accept the consequences of the pain, trusting God to deal with the offender.

3) Forgive from the heart by being real about the pain you felt.
4) Forgiveness does not let the person off the hook for what he or she did, nor does it condone his or her behavior. The pain you felt is real and valid.

Repentance: Repentance throughout the Bible is a call to surrender to God in every area of our lives. It is the act of asking God to forgive you after the Holy Spirit reveals a sin you have committed. You think about what you have done, how it hurts God or other people, and you go to God with a humble heart and repent for the behavior. The Bible says in 1 John 1:9, "If we confess our sins, he is faithful and just and will forgive us our sins and purify us from all unrighteousness." Acts 3:19 says, "Repent, then, and turn to God, so that your sins may be wiped out, that times of refreshing may come from the Lord." God promises to respond to our repentant hearts and gives us the power to get up and walk in a different direction. It's the action of making a literal U-turn! We repent for our sins when we ask Jesus into our hearts but also throughout our lives as Christ followers. His kindness and love should lead us to be lifetime repenters. Each time we repent, He cleanses our hearts, giving the Holy Spirit more authority in our lives.

Soul Ties: As a clinician, I was not aware of the power of ungodly soul ties that exist between two people whose relationship was based on hurt, rejection, or ungodly choices. God's desires and plan for our lives include relationships that honor Him and are loving and healthy with others. Unfortunately, the relationships and experiences we walk through in our lives are vulnerable to our flesh and this fallen world. I have come to understand that God's design for relationships to be pure and healthy is a way to protect us from harm, much like we set boundaries in our own lives.

I want you to think about the wounds of this relationship causing a tie that tightly binds you together on a spiritual level. This connection becomes an invitation for us to walk in the hurt and lies of this unhealthy bond many times, long after the relationship has ended. This tie creates a literal stronghold or wall that blocks the truth and God's perfect love from covering the pain and our hearts completely. Another way of understanding this is to recognize that this person and the harm he or she caused you can get between you and God. It is a strong tie that creates an open door for the enemy to speak lies and doubt about your identity and worth. This soul tie speaks into your heart and keeps you from receiving and fully believing that the blood of Jesus is enough. You know Him, perhaps, but the tie keeps you from total and complete submission to His truth and love. I would like for you to consider the relationships in your life that continue to cause pain that seems to have you stuck. These are the places that you know

God's truth but you still feel controlled by the words or behavior of a person, many times from years past. Now that you are able to look more deeply inside yourself, you can now see these ties more clearly. It is simply an opportunity to place the cross of Jesus between the pain and lies that you experienced with this person. This process invites Jesus's truth and love to become your filter and voice of truth in your life.

Many years ago, God gave me a vision, a picture of Jesus and my broken heart. I was walking down many roads of my life, and as I walked, I was tightly holding onto Jesus. It seemed like the journey was rugged and very long, but it involved restoration. I saw very clearly Jesus taking me from place to place where my heart had been shattered. At each place, we stopped, and He looked at me in a way as to say, "I felt your pain." He was acknowledging the depth to which it had affected me. I could remember them each so vividly. He then reached His nail-scarred hand into this memory and took back the piece of my heart that had been left behind in that painful place. He handed it to me, and then I put it back where it belonged. It was this incredible journey of Jesus completely healing my broken spirit and heart. I will never forget that vision and share it often as I describe God's desire to radically heal everything that has crushed our spirits.

Principle 4: Homework

1) Discuss the places you have struggled with for-giveness. Make a list of those who you need to forgive; ask God to show you who those people are. Then go to God and forgive them for the things they have done and, most importantly, the way they made you feel.

_____

_____

_____

2) Are there places in your life where you need to repent? Does this come easily for you? Ask God to reveal these places so He can forgive you.

_____

_____

_____

3) Are there people/wounds in your life that seem to be tied in an ungodly soul tie?

_____

_____

_____

In other words, do you still find yourself struggling with the pain in these relationships, even years later? Identify these and ask God to break them in Jesus's name.

_____

_____

_____

*Prayer to Break Soul Tie (see Appendix)

*Forgiveness Template (see Appendix)

Prayer:

> Lord, You are a loving and merciful God. I think about all the times I have turned away from You and the harm I may have caused other people throughout my life. Reveal to me any areas in my life where I need to repent. Give me a humble and teachable heart. Teach me how to be gracious and forgiving toward everyone, even those who do not take ownership for the pain they have caused me. I want to walk like You, Jesus! I thank you for forgiving me and washing me clean with Your blood on the cross. In Jesus's name, Amen.

Declaration:

I will be a man who actively chooses to forgive others as You have forgiven me. Teach me to let go of offense quickly and completely so I can walk purely before You every day of my life. Thank you that by Your death on the cross, I am healed and my sins are remembered no more! I thank you that because of this forgiveness, my chains are broken, and I am set free!

STRIPPED away

Matthew 6:14-15, Ephesians 4:31-32, 2
Corinthians 2:10-11

PRINCIPLE 5: SURRENDER: YES, LORD, I WILL GIVE YOU EVERYTHING

~~

Surrender definition: cease resistance and submit to authority.

Spiritual surrender: To completely give up your own will and subject your thoughts, ideas, and deeds to the will and teachings of God.

Rick Warren contends, "Surrender is not the best way to live; it is the only way to live. Nothing else works."(Warren 2019)

So let's get this straight. God is a jealous God, and He wants every part of us. This is not because He is mean or controlling but because He loves us so much. He knows anything less than His perfect love will not satisfy or give us the peace that He longs for His children to experience. A dear lady of faith told me years ago, "You can't have one leg over either side of the fence. A little church, a little time in the word—no, the world is too evil. You must be all in, or you will not survive." I remember hearing this many years ago and thinking, *God, I have a long way to go!* God sacrificed His Son and bought us, along with our shame, sin, and brokenness, with His blood to redeem us out of the hands of the enemy and assure that we would live a life worthy of our calling. He literally gave His life in return for ours.

There is young man in my community named Bruce Gilly who passed away nearly twenty years ago. His family continues to work for the kingdom in his memory. They use the words he always spoke in life as their mission statement, "Because He died for me, I will live for Him!" I love this statement! I have many times felt like my actions sent a message to God, saying "I know You sent Your Son, but I really have got this. I can handle this. I am too busy—really, have You seen all the things I have to deal with? I am tired. I mean, come on, God—You want everything from me?" The answer is a loud and resounding, "Yes, My child, everything." I heard one time that just maybe if Jesus could have one more nail driven into His body, maybe that would cause me to humble myself and give Him my life. The thought makes me feel ashamed, but I lived this way for many years.

I really did not understand what full surrender looked like. Several years ago, I was approached by a man with a message from God for me. He came up to me at a graduation party, never having met me before, and said, "I need to pray for you!" At the end of the night, he proceeded to tell me that although I had been on my knees in prayer for many years, I had failed to roll everything over onto the Lord. I would give Him a little bit but then get back up with the baggage still strapped to my back, much like a camel in biblical days as people moved from city to city. They would pack its back, and when they arrived at their destination, it would have to kneel so they could remove the supplies off its back.

Well, the fact is that even when the camel was on its knees, the packs were unreachable. The camel would literally have to roll over for all the burdens to come off! The truth is I did not fully trust God with my life. I knew He was my Creator, but I believed I had a better idea about what I needed in order to function and have a full life. I was holding onto my best and trying to carry the burdens on my own shoulders. He wrote the manual for my life, but I thought I knew best. Thank you, God, for the grace and mercy You have shown me over the years.

As we have talked about in earlier lessons, I had so many counterfeit things that I used to cover me, numb me, and tell me I could carry the weight that there was very little room left for God. He wanted to come deeply into my life and truly set me free with His truth. You see, if you hold onto other things, you do not have room to hold onto Jesus. Your hands are so full that one more thing will topple you over. The enemy has a plan to hijack you and keep your hands full with so much distraction, keeping you focused on lesser things, while he whispers the old lies over and over. While the enemy was trying to destroy us, God was pursuing us, running after us, leaving the ninety-nine to find us! (Matt. 8:12). He knew that we would get weary in survival and would eventually fall under the weight of all we were trying to carry. God knew, and He waited! He knew that we were created to serve Him and that eventually, we would cry out to Him in desperation.

I began to get very weary and cry out to Him in the midst of a difficult marriage and parenting teenagers. I was so tired and frustrated and could not seem to find any relief. By the grace of God and the fact that I am a rule follower, I did not run away from my circumstances. I spent countless nights on the floor crying out to God, "I give up. I can't take this pain. Please do something, anything, with my life!" It was then when I came to the end of myself, when I ran out of options and could no longer survive, that I laid my whole life down to Jesus. I rolled over, rolled everything onto the Lord, because I could no longer carry it. I really did not know what else to do! That was about four years ago. Oh, I had been gradually giving Him everything over the last twenty years, but the weight of my burden was still stacked high upon my back. But on that day, I threw in the towel and had nothing left.

I realize in hindsight He had been drawing me into surrender for many, many years. Surrender, a word that I saw as weakness and giving up, turned out to be the very posture that liberated and transformed everything in my life. Now the journey has been piece by piece, handing over everything. I made the vow to give Him everything, but the process has been lengthy. I was holding on pretty tightly to this world! I was putting my hope in so many lesser things. I built my life around all the survival tools, really not understanding what it means to let go and just abide in Jesus. Jesus said in Matthew, Mark, Luke, and John (you think it might be important since He included it in all the gospels?):

For if you want to save your own life, you will lose it; but if you lose your life for Christ you will save it. (Matthew 10:39, Mark 8:35, Luke 9:24, John 12:25).

Really letting go and surrendering actually gives you the freedom to live in the fullness of what God created you for—to live, love, give, serve, and walk in complete freedom and abundance. It's always a paradigm shift with God. Everything else in this life we feel led to accomplish or do, we set our minds to it and make it happen. With God, however, He just wants leaps of faith, walking day by day in complete dependency on Him for everything. In fact, everything that He asks us to do or we need to live purpose-driven lives requires laying aside all of our efforts and just being led by the Holy Spirit. You see, we are not trying to do anything. God has gone before us, and it is done—we just have to step into it and claim it! Believe me, I have tried hanging onto Jesus and myself, and it is a constant push and pull. My flesh demands attention while the Spirit beckons me to let Him lead me. It is like two hands on the steering wheel, one turning toward the right, one toward the left, with certain destruction ahead. One set of hands must come off the wheel in order to straighten up the car; literally let Jesus take the wheel. It really does feel good to let go, but that process can be one of much resistance and back-and-forth movement. I tell young people, just let Jesus drive. Take your hands off the wheel early so you don't have to wreck the car so many times! Everything that you give to God, He will give you peace and joy in its place. The more you let go, the more free you become. It really is an opposite mindset when we are seeking God with our whole hearts. This does not imply you are lazy and unmotivated; it just allows for you to hear your instructions from God then go to work extending His kingdom, following His directives, not your own thinking.

Martin Luther, who was a catalyst to Christianity in many ways, recalled, "I did nothing: the Word of God did everything." (Luther 2009).

The next steps involve really being honest with yourself and in prayer. Ask God to show you what you are still holding onto—past wounds, places, people, resources you have not given to Him or invited Him to have authority over.

Principle 5: Homework

1) Have you ever considered the idea of surrender as a positive step in your relationship with God? Does the idea of going all in with God scare you? Excite you?

_____

_____

_____

2) What are you still holding onto? What are you willing to surrender today to God? Take a few moments and give it to Him.

_____

_____

_____

Prayer

> Lord Jesus, I am ready now to let go and give You my life completely. I will no longer hold onto beliefs about myself that are less than what You say about me. I choose to give You my painful past, my current circumstances, and my plans for the future. My only hope is in You, Lord! I give up my life now so that I may live a life of purpose and abundance, fully trusting and fully surrendered to You each step of the way. In Jesus's name, Amen.

Declaration:

I will stand strong as a man of faith, understanding that my strength comes from fully surrendering my life to You. I will walk in victory by letting go of my life and becoming fully dependent on You. I will allow the Lord to examine my heart daily and reveal any area that I have not let go completely. I ask You, Lord, to strip away everything that keeps me from my true identity in Christ.

Matthew 16:24-25, Mark 10:28, Psalm 139:23-25

PRINCIPLE 6: LEARNING TO ABIDE: REMAINING IN HIS PERFECT LOVE

Abide: To endure without yielding; to await, to encounter; to remain stable and fixed. (Merriam-Webster's dictionary 2019).

From as far back as I can remember, I believed deep down that I must prove myself and that anything of value must be earned. That seemed to be the advice from most of the people I respected in my life. I spent most of my life trying to gain approval and looking for others' validation and respect. I did not realize that my Heavenly Father had given me a gift and invited me to just come into His presence and that He accepted me and loved me just the way I am. I think about all the years I did life from a place of trying and striving, doing and accomplishing, while holding onto the hand of Jesus. What I realize now is that He was gently calling my name and allowing me to get more weary and exhausted. He knew I would need to get to the end of myself to cry out for Him to help me. He began to whisper, "Let it go," asking me, "Will you give Me this? Will you trust Me with that?" Each question, each request, I longed to answer with a resounding yes. I said, "Yes, Lord!" What I have found now after several years of pursuing stillness is that it is a process. Letting go of self and my own will has been the most freeing and difficult thing I have ever done.

I watched a short video snippet several years ago with Pastor Tony Evans. He gave this beautiful analogy of abiding with his afternoon tea. He talked about how people put the tea bag into the hot cup of water and dunk it back and forth, up and down, up and down, then squeeze it inside the cup, then around and around again! Then they take the tea bag out, breathe a sigh of relief after the workout, and have a perfect cup of tea! It makes me tired just thinking about it. He said, "You know what I do? I get a cup of hot water. I gently drop the tea bag into the steeping hot water, and I let it steep and rest in the cup for a couple of minutes. No effort, no force, just let it abide! After about two minutes, I gently lift the tea bag out, and I have a perfect cup of tea." Wow, that hit me right between the eyes.

That word, *abide*! I was not sure exactly what it meant, but I knew it was important for me to understand.

I began to dig into Scripture and found the verses in John that talk about the vine and the branches. I had read these verses many times, but I really dug into them with my whole heart (John 15:1-8). You see, we are the branches, Jesus is the Vine, and God is the Vinekeeper. God tends to the vine and cares for the branches by pruning (stripping away) them regularly so they can produce good fruit. The good fruit He is talking about are the fruits of the Spirit—love, joy, peace, patience, kindness, goodness, faithfulness, gentleness, and self-control. God wants you to produce good fruit and will prune you and refine you until the fruit is sweet and abundant. This sounds wonderful, and it is, but the pruning process can be quite painful but very necessary. You see, our job as branches is just to stay connected to the Vine (Jesus)—nothing more, nothing less. We are called to abide (remain) in Him, and He will remain in us. The Word actually says if we abide in Christ that fruitfulness will stream from within us. He says that you can ask whatever you desire in His name and it will be done for you. (John 14:14)

The key for us is to learn to abide in Him and stop the constant striving that we have been taught our entire lives. You see, the union with Christ depends only on His grace and does not rest on anything we do or don't do! We are called to abide in Christ by allowing His Word to fill our hearts and minds. This empowerment by His grace will motivate and launch us into action that is divinely led. We learn to listen to God then work like crazy to complete the assignment He gives us. Abiding and being still means we stop fighting, we allow the Holy Spirit to direct our will, and we rest in the love of our Heavenly Father. He asks for our whole lives and requires obedience to complete the work that He has planned for each of us. So here's the truth—we can only abide when we remain in God's presence. The hardest part for me has been to let go of my own ideas and my own thinking in order to rest and receive from the Holy Spirit. It seems to be a daily push and pull, with my body and mind, flesh and spirit, to see who will take charge today. My decision has been made, my life has been yielded, but the process of learning to abide has been such a continual process.

I had an encounter with God recently where He met me in the kitchen early in the morning. I got my cup of coffee, which is the first order of business after I wake up. As I walked over to my table to begin my quiet time, He delivered a message to my heart. As I was holding my steaming cup of coffee, He said, "Your thinking is like that coffee cup, and My love and promises for your life are like the ocean, limitless and uncontainable. Every time you try to put My ocean in your coffee cup, you get overwhelmed, fearful, and confused, and you forget what I have spoken to you!" I love the way the Lord communicated in a way that I could understand. I have a deep love for the ocean and find it to be the most beautiful and majestic place as I watch the magnificence of the sea. He spoke very personally to my thinking, understanding that I had used my analytical thinking (overthinking) as a way to negotiate my life since I could remember. This was such a personal and profound truth from my Father. When I shared it with a friend, she said, "You know what you need to do? You need to throw that coffee cup into the ocean." So on my next trip to the beach, I did just that! What a moment of freedom as that cup went sailing into the sea! When I made the decision to throw my analytical thinking into the sea, I began to realize that this was not a one-time decision. It was a decision that I had to make every day for the rest of my life. My will or His, my life or His, my coffee cup or His ocean. He desires daily communion with me, and He desires for me to choose Him every day. I found that if I leaned on my own thinking and understanding, I would quickly veer outside of His presence. It is only in His presence that I am whole and complete. In His presence, I find my true identity and who He has called me to be. Truly, I have found that nothing satisfies a heart like being in the presence of Jesus.

Perfect Love: This concept is truly new to me. I never understood what love was until I began to understand the exchange that took place at the cross. My life for His, His body broken for me. Why? Just because He loved me! I knew love but not that kind of love—the kind of love that would leave heaven to find me and sacrifice His only Son on a wooden cross for me. Me! I had paid very little attention to Him for so many years. I was simply going about my busy day, living this life that He had died to give me. When I think about how much He suffered for me, it takes my breath away. I don't think any of us have a concept of what perfect love looks like until we read about Jesus' body being beaten for us while we were still sinners. I don't know exactly when or where it happened, but I saw His face, and I recognized what He did! I had no idea that love could be so selfless and purely based on His goodness and not about anything I did to earn or deserve it. I never knew that existed. As the walls around my heart began to fall, I was able for the first time to receive, rest, and experience His love. It was available always, but I had had so many guards up that I could not receive it or let Him love me. I think about all the counterfeit places we look for love and validation because we have never experienced the real thing. A forgery expert always recognizes the counterfeit because he or she has studied the authentic.

Change Your Awareness: How to Be Still in His Presence

To be mindful of something means to intentionally focus on the present. It means to pay attention to our thoughts and feelings without any judgement. Simply put it is giving oneself permission to observe. In other words, mindfulness is saying to self in a moment that there is no right or wrong way to think or feel; it's just practicing being present. You are present with God, your senses, your body, your thoughts, your feelings, and your current environment. You are not trying to stop distracting thoughts but just let them come and go out of your mind while you focus on being still. The goal is to bring your entire self into alignment with God. Paul tells Christians to be mindful of their relationship with Christ and to live in the present (Phil. 2:1-5).

Our left brain is the part of our brains that includes facts, logic, and mathematical thinking. This part of the brain uses reasoning and analysis to negotiate a given situation or to solve a problem. It is about containment and measurement and is very rational in nature. It is also the place where memories of past pain and responses to hurt and trauma exist. It keeps a record of the wrongs that have occurred and plays them over and over every day in our thinking.

Trauma: Deep pain and suffering is experienced in our psyches as trauma. Trauma changes brain chemistry, altering the very nature and design that our Creator has for our brains. This rewiring actually makes it impossible to think clearly and rationally at times. The part of our brains that is responsible to regulate feelings becomes so shut down that we feel defenseless and powerless much of the time. The trauma tells us to run and flee from vulnerability and to trust no one, especially God! It does not just say this—it announces it whenever we get triggered or feel overwhelmed. There is always a negative belief that is deeply embedded in the trauma. When Jesus arrives and is invited in, He whispers the truth about His protection, love, and ability to use the very pain to transform us and restore our hope. This statement is not logical or sensible; it is spiritual.

If we take our thoughts captive by identifying the lies and replacing them with God's truths from His Word, we can create change, overriding old neural pathways and renewing our minds! Unfortunately, for many of us, the thoughts are so rapid and filled with fear that it seems impossible to actually slow them down.

The right brain, however, is the side which controls creativity, imagination, dreams, and emotion. This is the part of the brain that allows us to be present in nature, worship, and relaxation. Music/Worship moves us to the right side of the brain. When we are listening to a song, it bypasses our logical thinking and allows us to be moved by the melody or the lyrics on a deep heart level. In 2 Kings 3:15-16, Elisha said, "Bring me a musician, so I can hear the voice of God." This, I believe, is an example of needing to be in a place that would allow him to hear God past his own logical thinking and understanding.

Learning to be mindful takes some practice and will require intentionality, but I can't think of anything that will provide more peace than this practice. This healthy coping behavior serves to keep ourselves filled with the Holy Spirit by keeping us in His presence. We have spent time in the earlier chapters emptying out the cup of pain and counterfeit coping; now we must keep the cup filled with the Holy Spirit through healthy coping practices:

Listening to Scripture

Bible reading

Prayer

Nature

Relaxation

Worship

All of these activities serve to ground us in the present moment, decrease emotional reactivity, and improve concentration and focus. These practices bring us back to center and escort us into the presence of God, helping us be more present with ourselves and leading us to know God in a more deep and meaningful way.

I would recommend starting out with 15-20 minutes of quiet time with the Lord. This time can include worship music, taking a walk and looking for God in nature, reading a section of Scripture, or just some deep, intentional breathing. These activities will escort you into the presence of God and a place of stillness and abiding. As you cultivate these habits of being still, increase the amount of time you spend and be intentional about doing them throughout the day. These simple efforts will draw you into a closer, more connected relationship with God. They will also reduce stress and increase your capacity for connection with other people.

Principle 6: Homework

1) Have you ever thought about the idea of abiding in Christ? Read John 15:1-8 and write about what it is saying to you.

_____

_____

2) Are you willing to be intentional about being in the presence of God? Remember that these habits will override fear and shame-based thinking, allowing you to be more responsive and present with God and the people in your life. Will you write a commitment below to practice 15-20 minutes of these habits each day?

_____

_____

_____

Prayer:

> Lord Jesus, I thank you that You pro-
> vided everything I need on the cross. I
> thank you that You have done the work
> and paid the price for all my past mis-
> takes and pain. Teach me, God, how to
> be mindful and still in Your presence. I
> need You to show me how to abide by
> the leading of Your Holy Spirit. I am a
> doer and a problem-solver, but I want
> to learn to rest in Your promises and
> walk in my true identity in Christ.

In Jesus's name, Amen.

Declaration:

I will be a man who is sold out to Jesus, fully surrendered and remaining in constant communication with
my Heavenly Father. Teach me, Lord, to tune out the
distractions and lesser things of this world that steal
my attention and affection away from You. I want to
learn to quiet my thinking, cease my striving, and abide
in Your presence.

Exodus 14:14, John 15:4-7, Psalms 131:1-2, Psalms 46:10

PRINCIPLE 7: YOU ARE LIVING PROOF: DEMOLISHING SHAME AND RECLAIMING THE POWER OF YOUR TESTIMONY

Y ou are the evidence, living proof that God is able to do what He says He will do! You are the proof that God can restore even the most broken vessel.

To testify is to tell the truth of what God has done in your life.

> "Be steadfast, immovable, always abounding in the work of the Lord" (1 Cor. 15:58).

> "Put on the whole Armor of God, so that
> you will be able to stand firm against
> the schemes of the devil" (Eph. 6:11).

In 1947, Chuck Yeager flew the Bell X-1 rocket 700 mph and became the first pilot to break the sound barrier.

Pilots in the past had attempted to break the barrier, but when they would enter into the compressibility region, there would be violent shaking caused by the sound waves. This shaking would cause the pilot to slow down, resulting in increased chaos. The natural tendency to slow down actually resulted in many pilots deaths while attempting this feat. Chuck Yeager had studied this and believed that if he went faster, it would quite possibly get him past the sound barrier. This turned out to be true! When he went faster and gave it everything he had, he was able to successfully break through the barrier. The faster he went through the resistance, the smoother the ride! He said, "It was as smooth as a baby's bottom; Grandma could be sitting up there sipping lemonade." (Yeager 2019)

He knew that just before breaking through the barrier he could anticipate the greatest resistance. He recognized it, planned for it, and pushed through it.

This reminds me of our lives on this earth. We have a tendency to give up hope and have so much anxiety when our lives begin to shake violently. If we can learn from Chuck's example to not lose hope but to stay to the course and draw closer to Jesus during these times, I believe we will experience a breakthrough as well. I have often heard that the one who gets the prize is the one who does not give up! God tells us in 1 Corinthians 9:24, "Did you not know that all runners run, but only one gets the prize? Run in a way as to get the prize." I think about this as instruction to not give up, to endure, and to push through. Those of us who practice abiding with Christ and stay focused and intentional will finish the race well.

My boys play hockey, and one of the sayings they would often use is a quote by the great Wayne Gretsky, "You miss 100% of the shots you don't take."(Gretsky 2014). Only those who endure, push through the resistance, and keep showing up will receive the prize.

Shame: This is a dark and daunting feeling. Melody Beattie defines shame as "an overwhelming negative sense that who we are isn't okay." (Beattie 1990). Shame can propel us deeper into self-defeating and sometimes self-destructive behaviors. Guilt is when we do something wrong, but shame implies that *who* we are is wrong. It is no wonder that the enemy does everything in his power to keep us in the bondage of shame and doubt. His agenda is to destroy our identity in Christ and to keep us from bearing fruit in the kingdom. He will use all his weapons to stop us from telling others about God's redeeming love. He deliberately and intentionally sets out to keep us from sharing our testimonies by whispering lies that keep us walking with our heads down in shame.

Not on our watch!

The Word of God talks about shame in several verses. In Romans 10:11, God says that if anyone believes in Him, he will never be put to shame.

In Revelation 12:11, God tells us that the enemy is defeated in two ways, by the blood of Jesus and the word of our testimony. So we overcome shame by believing the truth of what God says about us. To know what God says about us, we have to read the Bible. The Bible tells us that the Word of God is a razor-sharp sword that cuts through darkness, specifically the lies of the enemy.

In another translation, the Bible says, "They triumphed over the enemy by the blood of the Lamb and by the word of their testimony." (Revelation 12:11).

So let's break that down.

You overcome the evil one by the blood of Jesus and by sharing the story of your life and how God saved you and met you in the dark places. There is no testimony without a test. What if every believer was willing to tell his or her God story?

Now that's what I call revival! When this truth is actually walked out and becomes a normal part of being a Christ follower, think about all the people who would be set free. Then the power of shame would be demolished. Now that would set a family, church, and nation on fire!

It is my hope that we all take back the weapon by being willing to be vulnerable and transparent about our pasts and weaknesses. It's in these very places that God meets us and His power is made evident in our lives. Let's claim and walk in the *dunamis* power of the Holy Spirit! *Dunamis* is a Greek word referring to strength, power, or ability that is used numerous times in the New Testament. It is where the word dynamite comes from!

It does not reference just any power but miraculous power or marvelous works.

Key verses that reference this dunamis power are the following:

Mark 5:30; Luke 9:1, Luke 4:36, Luke 1:35, Acts 1:8, Ephesians 3:16, Psalms 131:1-2, Psalms 46:10

It is an inherit power that resides in us through our relationship with Christ. It is the empowerment through grace to have explosive power from the Holy Spirit acting in our lives. This explosive power gives us the ability to speak truth to others and lead them to Christ.

Mark Batterson says in his book *All In,* "The Gospel is a daring plan, not an insurance policy. He did not die to keep us safe, He died to make us dangerous! The gospel costs nothing but demands everything. If Jesus is not Lord of all, He is not Lord at all. It's all or nothing. It's now or never. It's time to up the ante and go all in with God!" (Batterson 2013).

Shame, as mentioned before, is an emotion that tells us that we are not okay. Melody Beattie says, "If it is dark and makes you feel bad about yourself, it's shame." (Beattie 1990). When I think about the pain Jesus endured in His death as He was beaten and His blood poured out, I always think about my shame being nailed to the cross. In other words, His death was enough! The nails were enough, the suffering was enough. I refuse to continue to carry the shame when He gave His life to set me free from it. I want you to again think about the exchange that took place on the cross—the exchange of our sin, pain, choices, and burdens for His life. In return, He gave us His righteousness and holiness. He literally paid the price for us so we would never have to carry this burden again. He knew we could not bear this weight and that we could never accomplish this on our own. Oh, what a Savior!

This past year, I heard Kirk Cameron speak at my church about the act of regeneration. This word is defined as spiritual renewal or revival. It bears the idea of a new birth or resurrection (raising from death to life). This is what happens when we ask Jesus into our lives. The enemy will use our lives before regeneration as evidence that we are hopeless and will never change. The whole idea of the gospel is that we were broken beyond repair and needed a Savior to bring us into right standing with the Lord. Why is it that we believe we should be righteous and good enough on our own? This belief opposes the exchange that Jesus made when He died for us. If we are okay and good enough, then why would we need a Savior? This understanding of regeneration really helps me move toward vulnerability, allowing me to let go of the fear and lie of shame. Why, yes, I was broken, ashamed, and guilty, but now I am born again and walk as a new creation in Christ.

Testimony: A testimony is a story about moving from death to life. This is a way to share the gospel with others by sharing your story of salvation. It gives others a personal example and story of how God can change one person's life.

Your testimony is a story of being rescued from the pit, forgiven, reconciled back to the Father, and walking as a new man. This is typically divided into three parts:

1) Your life before Christ
2) How you came to Christ (most emphasis on this part)
3) Life after you gave your life to Christ

Practical Steps for Sharing Your Testimony

1) Tell WHAT life was like for you before you knew Christ, who you were before you said yes and gave your heart to Jesus. This step is challenging because people tend to talk about their testimonies in two ways:

I have so much shame because I did terrible, ungodly things that I would never want people to know about me! Or

I have had a pretty good life—why would my story really impact anybody?

We tend to have been taught that in order to have a great powerful testimony, we must have been in the depths of pain and suffering. Although these stories can impact others in the same boat, the truth is that your individual story is the key to unlock the hearts of specific people. So there are some who may be called to share about freedom from drug addiction, while others may speak of Jesus's transforming power in their issues with low self-esteem or negativity. The enemy is always counting on you to overthink or disqualify your testimony.

The important part about this step is to be able to identify how you felt before you came to Christ. Some of the details of your brokenness can certainly be mentioned but should be kept at a minimum with the emphasis on how you felt during that time. I express this as before I found Jesus, I was overcome with fear and felt rejection very deeply in my heart. I used performance and pleasing people as a way to try to feel better and manage these emotions. I also share some of the desperate ways that I tried unsuccessfully to get the approval of people.

Take a few minutes now to do a mental inventory about what your life looked like before Christ.

2) The second step is to describe WHY and how you came to know Jesus. How did you feel? What happened to bring you into this relationship with God? What changed in your heart, and what difference did it make for your life? This step is really the most important because this is where you give hope to the person with

whom you are sharing your testimony. Your why could be the reason at that moment he or she decides to give his or her life to Christ.

For me, it was a gradual process of being set free from bondage. I was hurting and getting healthier but could not keep my joy and peace on my own. I got very tired and desperate and finally just waved a white flag and said, "I cannot do this anymore!" I felt like He said, "Good! Now maybe you will give things to Me." I said, "Yes, Lord, I don't want it anymore. I cannot carry it any longer—I want to give You everything!" I felt an immediate relief after I told Him I wanted to give Him my burdens; they were just so heavy.

This step is really important because it really tells of your encounter with God. Was it His kindness? Or did you experience His love in a way you could not resist? Or, like me, did you get so worn down and desperate that you just cried out to Him?

3) The last step is to talk about HOW life has changed since you became a new creation in Christ.

This step will be constantly changing as you walk more intentionally as a Christian. It starts with a declaration of faith, and then you begin a journey of walking with God. It is important to share how your life has been changing. What is He teaching you about His character and His ways? How are you growing and maturing in Christ? It is also important to describe new revelations or places of freedom you are currently experiencing.

For me, my life is radically changing. I have found that the more I run after God, the more I am transformed! As I seek Him with my whole heart, He is changing and renewing everything the enemy tried to steal in my life.

Principle 7: Homework

1) Have you fully understood the exchange that took place at the cross? It is important that you recognize you have a new identity in Christ; the old is gone, and you are completely new! How does this affect you and how you see yourself?

_____

_____

_____

2) Have you allowed the world and the enemy to compromise or keep you from sharing your testimony? Will you begin to take this powerful story to people around you? Discuss how you are willing to do this.

_____

Prayer:

> Thank you, God, for the way You love
> me. You went to the ends of the earth
> to rescue me from sin and the plans
> of the enemy. Give me courage and
> strength to stand as a mighty oak tree,
> strong and immovable in the face of
> struggle and pain. You are my Deliverer
> and my Hope in this world. I believe You
> created me to bear fruit, and I am the
> proof that even the most broken of sin-
> ners can be healed, redeemed, and set
> free. Give me boldness and focus as You
> use all of my story to change this world.
> In Jesus's name, Amen.

Declaration:

God, I am a man who values everything that You have
done for me. I have viewed myself from the eyes of this
world for the last time. I will be a man like David, who
discerned that he was king when he was still in the field,
unnoticed and rejected by his own father. He knew he

was being prepared and that every test and struggle would only serve to make him stronger. I refuse to walk in shame about my past mistakes! I stand now as a new creation in Christ. The old man is gone, and I am choosing to walk in my true identity, according to what God says about me. I will share my story with others as the Holy Spirit leads me. I believe that it is by the blood of the Lamb and the word of my testimony that people will be set free!

Revelation 12:11, 1 John 5:11, John 4:39

appendix

Group Leader Instructions

(suggested group size 4-8 men)

I am so thrilled that you are willing to gather some men together and jump into this study. I have done my best to include the information that you will need to launch this study in your living room, church, or office. I believe the principles presented will encourage healthiness and move you into a more intimate relationship with Jesus. The most meaningful part of this process is the opportunity to connect and be in community with other men. It is my hope that this study will be a catalyst to open, honest, and vulnerable sharing. I have found that there is nothing more powerful than walking shoulder to shoulder with other believers in a safe and trusting environment.

Suggested Group Structure and Outline

(I say suggested because you are free to let this be a guideline but defer to the Holy Spirit as He meets you in this process.) I think the group is best accomplished in a ten-week window. It is my hope that some of the members will feel convicted about leading a new group of men after the completion of this group.

I would suggest that you read through the weekly assigned principles several times to prepare for the upcoming group. Let the Lord speak to your heart and give you His strength as you lead this group.

Pray about the men you will invite and that they will come with teachable and open hearts. Pray weekly for your guys to be continually open and exposed.

Welcome/Introduction Group

+Begin with opening prayer.

+Welcome each person.

+Leader introduces self and discusses the reasons he has decided to lead this group.

+Who this study was written for:

They are mighty men, broken men, ground-breakers, overcomers, yielded to God, survivors, invested in healthiness, recovering, bold in their communities and churches, motivated to be strong men of God with teachable hearts, open to realignment, and having a desire to live out their calling and purpose.

+Set ground rules for safety and confidentiality.

What is said in group stays in group. (There can be no expectation for openness and vulnerability without trust.)

+Discuss that commitment to the ten weeks is very important, missing only if it is absolutely necessary, understanding that each principle and the relationships gain momentum with each week.

+Distribute books to each participant.

+Assign reading of the introduction and encourage each man to complete the assessment in the front of the book for the next week. Let them know that sharing of the assessment is optional but encouraged as a way to give permission to be transparent. However, if people do not want to share, this is a great tool for self-reflection.

Group #2

+Prayer/Welcome

+Ice-breaker suggestions:

(Who was your favorite teacher/coach? Why?)

(What is your favorite candy?)

(Tell about one hobby you have.)

+Worship

I suggest sharing a couple worship songs or hymns that you believe will speak the men in your group.

I like to introduce worship at this point in case others have never experienced this aspect of their walk with God. Instruct each person to do what feels comfortable to him (sit, stand, kneel). This may be a bit awkward for some people, so be sure to model the importance of showing honor and reverence to God in this way.

The idea with worship is to simply bring each person into the presence of God. It is an understanding that true worship is offering ourselves to God, learning to bow down before Him in reverence and respect, focusing on His goodness, and moving outside of our logical thinking.

+Discuss the introduction chapter, how it resonated with you, and then ask others to give their own personal feedback.

+Open the discussion about the assessment questions. Share a few things that you learned about yourself in this process. Encourage others and ask for volunteers to share.

+Assign Principle #1 to be completed for next week.

+Prayer/Praise requests

Give anyone who feels led to pray an opportunity, but always be willing to pray if no one volunteers.

Groups 3-9

+Welcome/Opening prayer

+Worship (songs, hymns, read selected scripture, moments of silence to just invite God into their hearts and this time together)

+Principle presented and discussed

+Go over homework for the week. I suggest this be done by dividing men into groups of two for more in-depth sharing. This is an experiential piece prompted by specific questions. These questions are designed to take the principle to a deeper, more personal level. (20-30 minutes)

+Group discussion about what resonated with each person after having time to share

+Prayer read aloud by one volunteer

+I would like to encourage each person to read the declaration individually and out loud. This is an announcement of intent to practice the given principle.

+Specific prayer requests/Needs of encouragement/ One thing you learned from this principle

+Assign the next chapter as homework.

*At the close of group #9, ask each participant to consider sharing a short five- minute testimony at the final group meeting. This is encouraged but not mandatory. Give the suggestion to follow the guidelines as discussed in the last principle.

Group #10

This final group provides an opportunity to share your testimony with the other members of your study group. This is a step of courage as a true believer. It is important to realize that your testimony is the key to unlocking the prison in someone else's life. You and your story are the proof of what God can do in one man's life.

Encourage and give each person the opportunity to tell his story using the format described in the last principle. It needs to be no more than about 5-8 minutes to allow each person a time to share.

Feelings List

ANGER

adamant	quarrelsome	diffident	prim
angry	rage	distracted	prissy
bitchy	righteous	distraught	queer
challenged	sneaky	dubious	relieved
combative	spiteful	embarrassed	remorseful
competitive	stingy	fawning	restless
cruel	superior	fearful	scared
deceitful	tempted	flustered	servile
destructive	tenacious	frightened	sheepish
determined	unnourished	guilty	shocked
envious	vehement	gullible	shy
envy	violent	helpless	skeptical
evil	whiney	homesick	solemn
frustrated	wicked	hopeless	sorrowful
fury		horrible	startled
greedy		hysterical	strange
grouchy	**FEAR**	intimidated	stunned
hate		isolated	stupefied
irritable	ambivalent	jealous	stupid
infuriated	annoyed	lazy	tense
lecherous	anxious	low	tentative
mad	apathetic	maudlin	tenuous
mean	bad	nervous	terrible
obnoxious	betrayed	overwhelmed	terrified
obsessed	bored	pain	threatened
opposed	captivated	panicked	tired
outraged	confused	persecuted	trapped
parsimonious	conspicuous	petrified	uneasy
pissed	contrite	pity	unsettled
	culpable	precarious	
	different		

GRIEF

abandoned
agony
bitter
burdened
cheated
condemned
crushed
defeated
despair
diminished
discontented
discouraged
disturbed
divided
dominated
empty
exasperated
foolish
frantic
grief
hurt
ignored
imposed upon
jumpy
left out
lonely
longing
melancholy
miserable

nutty
odd
pressured
rejected
sad
screwed up
suffering
thwarted
troubled
ugly
vulnerable
weepy
worried

JOY

adequate
affectionate
alert
almighty
astounded
awed
beautiful
blissful
bold
brave
calm
capable
charmed
cheerful

childish
clever
contented
delighted
desirous
eager
ecstatic
elated
electrified
enchanted
energetic
enervated
enjoy
excited
exhausted
fascinated
flirtation
foolish
free
full
gay
glad
good
gratified
groovy
happy
heavenly
helpful
high
honored

impressed
infatuated
inspired
hopeful
joyous
keen
kicky
kind
loving
lustful
naughty
nice
nutty
peaceful
pleasant
pleased
pretty
proud
rapture
refreshed
relaxed
relieved
reverent
rewarded
safe
sated
satisfied
secure
settled
sexy

silly
stuffed
sure
sympathetic
talkative
valued
vital
vivacious
wanted
wonderful
zany

OTHER

bored
cold
depressed
hungry
sleepy
thirsty
tired
war

Lids and Spouts Guide

Lids: These are coping behaviors/techniques that numb and medicate. They repress our pain and keep it locked deep inside. They keep us in denial and diminish the work of the Holy Spirit in our lives.

Lids: Alcohol, food, pornography, drugs, performance, people pleasing, control, manipulation, isolation, overthinking, procrastination, avoidance, distraction (phone, computer, TV).

Spouts: These are coping behaviors/techniques that expose and resolve the pain we experience. They encourage pouring out the lies and pain, leaving room for the Holy Spirit to come in and bring healing.

Spouts: Prayer, talking with a friend, reading the Bible, exercise, nature, music, worship, therapy, creativity, and journaling.

Soul Tie Prayer

> Lord, I recognize that I have an unhealthy soul tie with _____. I come into Your presence and would like to break this tie supernaturally. I forgive him/her for hurting me and repent for my part of this unhealthy relationship. I ask that You would stop the flow of anything ungodly between us, and I place the cross of Jesus between me and _____. I ask You to close every doorway in this relationship that the enemy has used to influence me and harm me. I thank you, God, for healing my heart. In Jesus's name, Amen.

Forgiveness Guide

Ask God to reveal to you all the people you need to forgive. I suggest making a list and following these steps with each person.

Pray the following prayer:

> I choose to forgive _____
> for_____(what he or she specifically did to harm you).
>
> It made me feel_____.
>
> I relinquish my right to revenge, and I turn him/her over to You, Lord.
>
> I now ask You to bless_____ (the person).
>
> In Jesus's name, Amen.

Letter to Your Little Boy

One of my favorite techniques for moving forward and letting go of pain is letter writing. In this exercise, you are given the opportunity to speak truth into your own life by sharing with yourself as a child. Think about what you wish someone had told you; what did you need most from your caregivers that you did not get? You can give those words and affirmations to yourself right now. As you write to the little boy, tell him about what you have learned over the years. In your own words, let him know that he is going to be okay and that he will survive the difficulties he is currently facing. This is a powerful exercise and creates such a bridge of connection between your head and heart.

You can begin the letter with Dear_____ (Your name),

Write down everything you want him to know, things you wish he knew back then, and the truth about who he will become. It may be as short as a paragraph or it might be pages; just let it flow.

Love, _____(Your name)

notes

1. *Merriam-Webster Online*, s.v. "restoration," accessed on September 29, 2019, https://www.merriam-webster.com/dictionary/restoration.

2. *Merriam-Webster Online*, s.v. "forgiveness," accessed on November 14, 2019, https://www.merriam-webster.com/thesaurus/forgiveness.

3. *Merriam-Webster Online*, s.v. "surrender," accessed on October 25, 2019, https://www.merriam-webster.com/thesaurus/surrender.

4. "Rick Warren Quote," LibQuotes, last modified 2020, https://libquotes.com/rick-warren/quote/lbt4v7j.

5. Martin Luther, "The Word Did It All," *ReformationTheology*, last modified March 20, 2009, http://www.reformationtheology.com/2009/03/the_word_did_it_all_martin_lut.php.

6. *Merriam-Webster Online*, s.v. "abide," accessed on December 16, 2019, https://www.merriam-webster.com/thesaurus/abide.

7. David Onkst, "Biography," *ChuckYeager.org*, last modified 2019, http://www.chuckyeager.org/history/background/.

8. Paul Brown, "'You Miss 100 Percent of the Shots You Don't Take.' You Need to Start Shooting at Your Goals," *Forbes*, last modified on January 12, 2014, https://www.forbes.com/sites/actiontrumpseverything/2014/01/12/you-miss-100-of-the-shots-you-dont-take-so-start-shooting-at-your-goal/#51132e256a40.

9. Mark Batterson, All In: You Are One Decision Away From a Totally Different Life (Grand Rapids, Michigan: Zondervan, 2013), 11, 21.

10. Melody Beattie, The Language of Letting Go: Daily Meditations on Codependency (Center City, Minnesota: Hazelden Publishing, 1990), 34.